Copyright © 2020 Hillsong International Ltd atf Hillsong International

First printed in Australia ©2012 by Hillsong Church Ltd.

All rights reserved. No part of this book may be reproduced in any form by any mechanical or electronic means including information storage or retrieval systems, without permission in writing from the publisher.

While the manual is consistent with the values of Hillsong, the program and manual are suitable for use within any value or faith-based system. The purpose of this community development program is to promote a holistic, humanitarian and strengths-based approach to life.

Enquiries should be addressed to the publishers.

Hillsong Music Australia, PO Box 1195, Castle Hill NSW 1765, Australia

T: +61 2 8853 5300
F: +61 2 8846 4625
E: resources@hillsong.com

WARNING:

The ShineGIRL Facilitator Handbook and ShineGIRL Journals are provided to help facilitate the running of the ShineGIRL program. Although the content of the program is copyright protected it does NOT constitute, or contain legal, medical or other advice. Use of this handbook and running the program is entirely at your own risk.

Before running this program, you should obtain your own legal, insurance and other professional advice in the State, Territory or Country in which you intend to run the program.

SHINE

MY **SHINEGIRL** JOURNAL

name & date

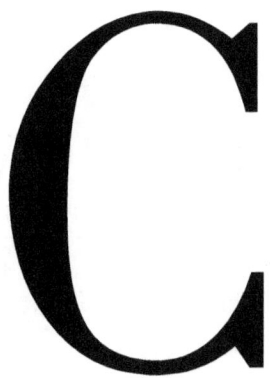

SHINEGIRL OVERVIEW SIX
SESSION ONE I AM VALUABLE ELEVEN
SESSION TWO I AM ONE-OF-A-KIND SEVENTEEN
SESSION THREE I AM WONDERFULLY MADE TWENTY-THREE
SESSION FOUR I HAVE THE POWER OF CHOICE THIRTY-ONE
SESSION FIVE MY DECISIONS DETERMINE MY DESTINATION THIRTY-SEVEN
SESSION SIX I HAVE RESILIENCE FORTY-NINE
SESSION SEVEN MY POTENTIAL IS LIMITLESS FIFTY-SEVEN
SESSION EIGHT MY LIFE HAS PURPOSE SIXTY-SEVEN
SESSION NINE SHINE! EIGHTY-ONE

overview.

ShineGIRL is a unique personal development and group mentoring tool that uses an inspirational, practical and experiential approach to learning. This program is founded upon the premise that every life counts and has intrinsic value, and fosters an awareness of this belief. As a result, girls are equipped to become effective global citizens for the future.

aim.

For each girl to develop understanding of her own personal worth, strength and purpose and realise the potential within her to fulfil her desires.

objectives.

Equip girls to:

Identify themselves as valuable with much to contribute to society
Build confidence and gain an understanding of intrinsic value
Develop decision-making and problem-solving skills
Understand they are able to have a positive influence in their world
Identify personal desires and strengths to motivate them to set and achieve personal goals

three foundational concepts. worth. strength. purpose.

i have WORTH!

'BODY AND SOUL, I AM WONDERFULLY MADE'

The focus for these sessions is for you to understand for yourself that you are valuable.
Your uniqueness is something to celebrate and you have been wonderfully made.

i have STRENGTH!

'CHOOSE LIFE'

These sessions explore the power of choice and the power that decisions have on shaping a person's future.
This is addressed through practical sessions about feelings, convictions, decision-making and problem-solving.

i have PURPOSE!

'I HAVE A HOPE AND A FUTURE'

Purpose is examined through exploring personal hopes, dreams and desires.
Goal setting, group discussions on potential talents and practical activities, are used to equip
and build confidence to live out a purpose-filled, adventurous life.

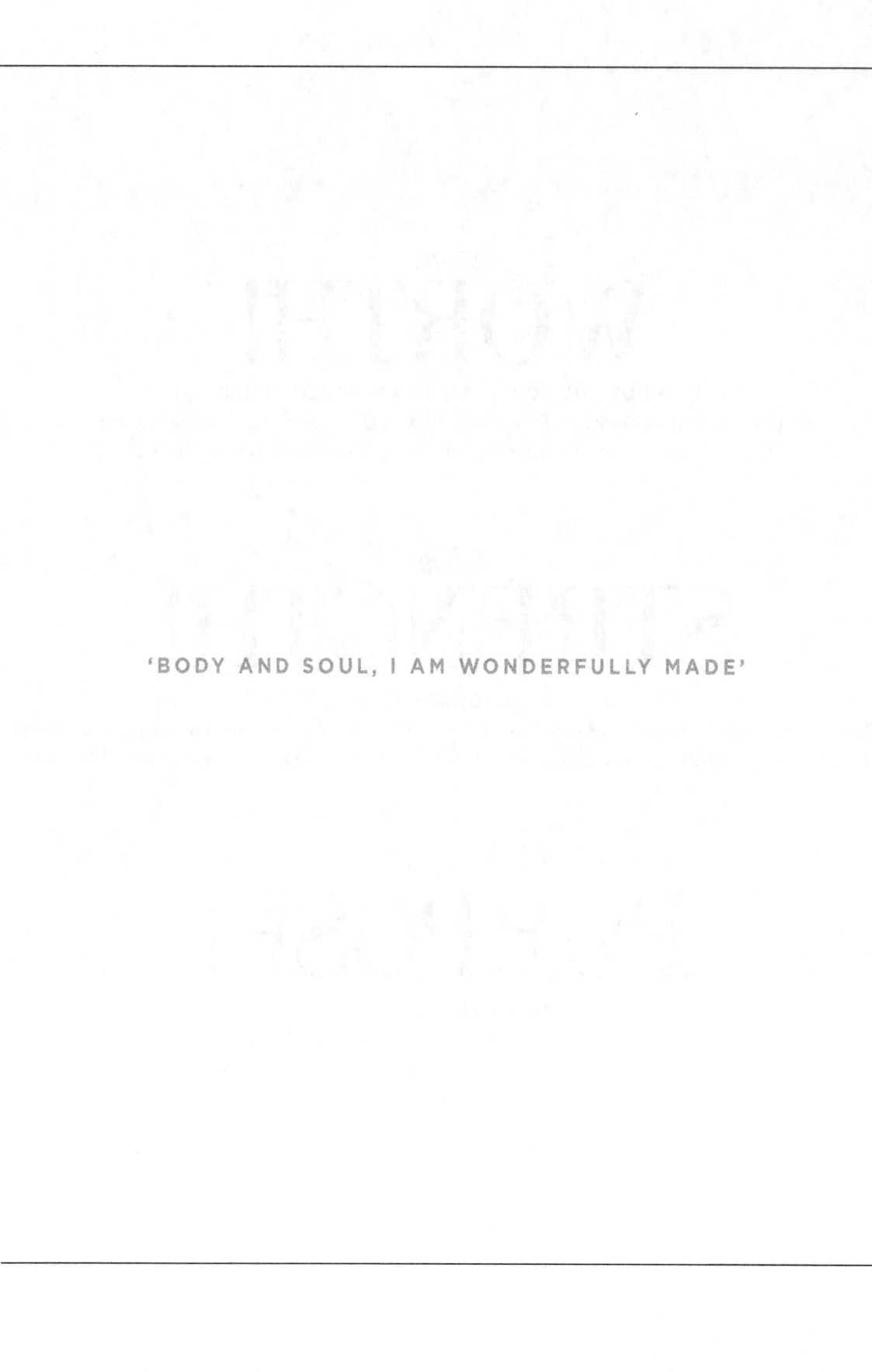

'BODY AND SOUL, I AM WONDERFULLY MADE'

W
worth.

SESSION ONE I AM VALUABLE
SESSION TWO I AM ONE-OF-A-KIND
SESSION THREE I AM WONDERFULLY MADE

1

worth.

SESSION ONE | I AM VALUABLE

outcomes.
By the end of this session, you will be able to:
GAIN AN UNDERSTANDING OF THE CONCEPT OF VALUE
IDENTIFY WHAT YOU PERSONALLY VALUE AND WHY
DEVELOP AN AWARENESS OF PERSONAL VALUE

foundational concept.

Our value has nothing to do with what we think or what people say about us. Our value is not attached to our performance. It is not based on our circumstances, family background, religion or socio-economic status. Human value is not determined by what people say about us. It's not determined by whether or not we have failed more times than we have succeeded. Our value is not determined by whether or not we have finished school, have a job, a car, are in a relationship or are popular. Circumstances such as if we are sick or healthy, rich or poor do not determine our value.

Our value is linked to our very being – it is intrinsic. Value cannot be earned, regardless of what circumstances we find ourselves in, we all qualify for value and worth. Explore the questions: 'Am I accepted? Do I matter? Do you see me? Do you hear me? Does what I am saying matter to you? Do you recognise me? Do your eyes light up when I am around?'

Every one of us has this need for acceptance. It's a universal need. You matter! What you have to say matters. You are worth being cared about, listened to and validated. You are recognised. You are important. Living a life of value embraces the (young) woman that is emerging and gives her space to grow. Puberty is an adventure and it only lasts for a short while.

ILLUSTRATION: OUR VALUE IS PRICELESS

Human value is not determined by what people say about us. It's not determined by whether or not we have failed more times than we have succeeded. Our value is not determined by whether or not we have finished school, have a job, a car, are in a relationship or are popular. Circumstances such as if we are sick or healthy, rich or poor do not determine our value.

reflection.
Q. How do hands relate to value?

_____
_____
_____
_____
_____
_____
_____

Q. What do we use our hands for?

_____
_____
_____
_____
_____
_____
_____

Q. What are some things hands can do for people – helping and giving?

_____
_____
_____
_____
_____
_____

Hands were never designed to cause harm to ourselves or to others. Hands are an extension of our gifts and talents into the world. Our hands are designed to serve us well and serve others well in love. A hurting humanity can end up having hands that hurt others, but it's not what our hands are meant to be doing.

Hands are only one part of our amazing body. They are never insignificant and add to our worth as a human being. Every hand not only looks unique and is one-of-a-kind, but every hand does unique things.

'BODY AND SOUL, I AM WONDERFULLY MADE'

2
worth.
SESSION TWO | I AM ONE-OF-A-KIND

outcomes.
By the end of this session, you will be able to:
RECOGNISE THE VALUE OF BEING ONE-OF-A-KIND.
DISTINGUISH THE DIFFERENCE BETWEEN UNIQUENESS AND COMPARISON.

one-of-a-kind is
BEAU TIFUL

Each of us was born with a one-of-a-kind personality. The way we love is one-of-a-kind. Our personal style and creativity is one-of-a-kind. How we communicate is different. How we write or give expression to something is unique. If a group of people were to write about the same topic, not one paper would be written the same. That is because our personal expression of life is unique and one-of-a-kind.

When something is one-of-a-kind, it is precious and valuable; it is a treasure... it has worth. Each of us is set apart as unique and there is no one like us! We are born one-of-a-kind, custom-built and a masterpiece!

UNIQUE

| *yoo*-neek |

A one-off, original, exceptional, rare, unequalled, extraordinary, incomparable, matchless, individual.

We are all different! This is something to celebrate.

DIFFERENT

| dif-er-*uh* nt |

Not the same, unlike, of other nature, form or quality.

reflection.

Q. How does my appearance give expression to my one-of-a-kind life?
___
___
___
___
___

Q. How does my heritage and culture give expression to my one-of-a-kind life?
___
___
___
___
___

Q. How does my personality and character give expression to my one-of-a-kind life?

Q. How does my personal written signature give expression to my one-of-a-kind life?

TWENTY-ONE I AM ONE-OF-A-KIND

'BODY AND SOUL, I AM WONDERFULLY MADE'

3

worth.

SESSION THREE I AM WONDERFULLY MADE

outcomes.
By the end of this session, you will be able to:
HAVE AN UNDERSTANDING OF THE WORTH CONCEPT.
IDENTIFY WAYS TO VALUE YOURSELF.

foundational concept.

There are many facets to who we are. Every part of us has a purpose and a function. Our mind, body, emotions, personality, character, passions and dreams are all intricate parts of who we are.

There are many characteristics that contribute to our individuality; our strengths, talents, laughter and smile have all been uniquely designed just for us. No one else is exactly the same. We have been designed just the way we are for a reason and a purpose.

The idea of living a life that shines is to see all that we do be about placing value on ourselves and others. We exercise to be strong in the core of our body so that we can be fit to carry on our amazing journey well. We require fuel for the body by eating the right food to keep healthy, as well as limiting chemicals where possible that are harmful for our inner and outer environment. So when we love something, we value it, anything we love and adore we treat with value. When we love ourselves, we are valuing ourselves.

we are all
PRICE LESS

ILLUSTRATION: A TEACUP STORY

A couple went into an antique shop one day and found a beautiful teacup sitting on a shelf. They took it off the shelf, so they could look at it more closely, and said, "We really want to buy this gorgeous cup."

All of the sudden, the teacup began to talk, saying, "I wasn't always like this. There was a time when I was just a cold, hard, colourless lump of clay. One day my master picked me up and said, 'I could do something with this.' Then he started to pat me, and roll me, and change my shape."

"I said, 'What are you doing? That hurts. I don't know if I want to look like this! Stop!' But he said, 'Not yet.'

"Then he put me on a wheel and began to spin me around and around and around, until I screamed, 'Let me off, I am getting dizzy!' 'Not yet,' he said.

"Then he shaped me into a cup and put me in a hot oven. I cried, 'Let me out! It's hot in here, I am suffocating.' But he just looked at me through that little glass window and smiled and said, 'Not yet.'

"When he took me out, I thought his work on me was over, but then he started to paint me. I couldn't believe what he did next. He put me back into the oven, and I said, 'You have to believe me, I can't stand this! Please let me out!' But he said, 'Not yet.'

"Finally, he took me out of the oven and set me up on a shelf where I thought he had forgotten me. Then one day he took me off the shelf and held me before a mirror. I couldn't believe my eyes, I had become a beautiful teacup that everyone wants to buy."

AUTHOR UNKNOWN

reflection.

Q. Do we truly value and appreciate our bodies?

_____
_____
_____
_____
_____
_____

Q. If our bodies are valuable to us, how should we look after them?

_____
_____
_____
_____
_____
_____
_____

'CHOOSE LIFE'

strength.

SESSION FOUR I HAVE THE POWER OF CHOICE
SESSION FIVE MY DECISIONS DETERMINE MY DESTINATION
SESSION SIX I HAVE RESILIENCE

strength.

SESSION FOUR I HAVE THE POWER OF CHOICE

outcomes.
By the end of this session, you will be able to:

EXPLORE AND UNDERSTAND THAT YOU WERE BORN WITH FEELINGS.
DEMONSTRATE SKILLS REQUIRED TO ENHANCE THE POWER OF CHOICE.

foundational concept.

We have a free will – the power to make choices in our lives. Strength comes when we make choices that benefit ourselves and others. Just like push-ups help build our physical strength, every time we make a good decision it is like doing a push-up for our soul. Inner strength comes from the daily decision to choose to do the right thing. And sometimes it can seem like there is no 'right choice'. It takes real strength in those situations to weigh up the consequences and make the best choice we can.

Choices affect our lives and the lives of people around us. No matter how we feel, we have the power to choose our direction in life. This does not mean choices will always be easy. Some of our choices will be challenging. Making right choices in life, especially in difficult situations, builds our strength and maturity as young girls. Our decisions can be influenced by others, especially those we love (family, friends, partners). For example, some teenage girls make decisions they regret because they feel pressured by their friends to do things they wouldn't normally do just so they can fit in. In situations like that we can choose to either hand our 'power of choice' over to others or hold onto it ourselves.

No matter what happens in life, whether we feel powerless or not,
we will always have the power of choice.

We have the CHOICE to:
RESPOND to a situation or REACT to it.

managing our emotions.

EMOTION | ih-moh-sh*uh* n |
Any strong feeling, such as joy or fear, the part of a person's character based on feelings rather than thought.
It's important to recognise how we are feeling.

Feelings are keys to revealing what we think about things - our mindsets, our belief systems. What we think and subsequently feel, influences the decisions we make and how we live out our life.

THOUGHTS & BELIEFS • FEELINGS • DECISIONS • RESPONSE

All these things influence our behaviours and actions.

Our thoughts and beliefs influence our feelings, which influence our decision-making. These in turn influence our responses to situations. It's important to maintain a balance when it comes to our emotions and not live a life controlled by them. Our emotions can become like a rollercoaster. If we allow our feelings to get out of balance they can begin to run our lives. In order to keep ourselves balanced we use our emotions to tell us how we are feeling, instead of allowing them to influence our choices in life.

Once we identify our feelings, it may be helpful to explore them further:

- Why am I feeling like this?
- What has caused these feelings?
- What choices do I have?
- Do I need to forgive someone?
- How can I resolve this?
- How long have I felt this way?
- Can I change how I am feeling?

For example: If you're feeling angry, ask yourself: Why am I angry? Where is this coming from? What has caused this anger? How long has this made me angry?

When we begin to explore our feelings and the reasons behind them, we start to understand our past and our present and look forward to a different future.

STRENGTH IS...
MAKING GOOD DECISIONS.

RECOGNISING OUR FEELINGS/EMOTIONS.

RESPECTING OURSELVES AND OTHERS.

BUILDING HEALTHY RELATIONSHIPS.

BEING OKAY WITH MAKING MISTAKES AS LONG AS WE LEARN FROM THEM.

LOOKING FOR THE GOOD IN ALL THINGS.

ASKING FOR HELP WHEN WE NEED IT.

BEING THANKFUL.

KNOWING WHAT WE STAND FOR.

CHOOSING TO ACCEPT AND LOVE OURSELVES FOR WHO WE ARE.

'CHOOSE LIFE'

strength.

SESSION FIVE MY DECISIONS DETERMINE MY DESTINATION

outcomes.
By the end of this session, you will be able to:
APPLY AND PRACTISE DECISION-MAKING AND PROBLEM-SOLVING SKILLS.
IDENTIFY WAYS TO DISPLAY RESPECT TO YOURSELF AND OTHERS.

foundational concept.

In every situation, in every day, we make choices. As a result of these choices there are consequences. Consequences will either cause us to move forward in life, stop us from moving at all or cause us to move backwards. There are decisions that can fast track us to our desired destination and others that can keep us from it.

Decisions we make give us control over our life, but they don't just affect our life, they also impact the people around us. Choices can be selfish or selfless.

Every decision we make – from getting out of bed each morning to choosing to arrive at school on time – has a consequence. Our choices impact what our tomorrow will look like. Things we decide to overcome and things we decide to accept all have a direct impact on our life. Often we don't realise that it's the small, everyday decisions that help us move towards our desired destination.

respect.

RESPECT | *ri*-spekt |
Esteem for or a sense of the worth or excellence of a person, the condition of being esteemed or honoured, to show regard or consideration for.

Q. How can we respect ourselves?

_____
_____
_____
_____
_____
_____
_____
_____

Q. What does respect look like for you?

_____
_____
_____
_____
_____
_____
_____
_____

Q. What are practical ways you can show respect to your fellow students and teachers?

_____
_____
_____
_____
_____
_____

Q. What can you do to display respect to yourself, your peers and your teachers or to your family this week?

_____
_____
_____
_____
_____
_____

BULLYING

Now that we have identified what respect looks like, what is the opposite of respecting someone? What does that look like?

Bullying is the opposite of respecting others. Bullying involves intentional acts of harmful behaviour towards another person and normally occurs where there is a power imbalance i.e. where a more powerful person (or people) usurp themselves over another person that they see to be less than. These behaviours include:

- Name-calling
- Physically fighting
- Victimization through ignoring or isolating
- Intimidation and/or harassment, and
- Cyber-bullying

Bullying is not generally a single event of inappropriate behaviour between equals.

CYBER-BULLYING

It is much easier to be more outgoing or provocative online. People find they can be personally more aggressive and forward than they are in 'real life' because they are hiding behind a computer screen or mobile phone However, what is being written, posted or sent does contribute to the real-life impression of who a person is seen to be.

Here are some types of cyber-bullying:
- Spreading rumours about people on social media, via text messages or online
- Accessing another person's account information, without permission, to see their details or to pretend to be them
- Sexting unsolicited photos or messages
- Trolling

Consequences of cyber-bullying can include:
- A plethora of negative effects on the recipient.
- Once circulated on the internet, it may never disappear. Info and images can be found at later times.
- What is posted online may have a negative effect on future applications for college or employment.
- Cyber-bullies may face legal charges. e.g. if the cyber-bullying is sexual in nature such as sexting.

Q. What is the difference between face-to-face bullying and cyber-bullying?

___
___
___
___
___
___

INVESTIGATE

Find some bullying statistics that are relevant to your local community. Record them here.

_____
_____
_____
_____
_____
_____
_____
_____
_____
_____
_____
_____
_____
_____
_____
_____
_____
_____
_____
_____
_____
_____

Q. What are some things you can do to help prevent bullying?

_____
_____
_____
_____
_____
_____
_____

CONVICTION | kuh n-vik-shuh n |
A fixed or firm, strong belief.

Convictions are what we believe is important to us. Convictions help us make decisions. Before we make a decision, we can think about whether it is in line with our convictions. There is a reason why we live with convictions. For example, I have a conviction to finish my education pathway because I want to get a good education and set myself up for the future. Convictions are formed from our beliefs and values. When we make decisions based on our convictions we are showing others what we believe and value in life.

Having personal convictions will make it easier for us to make the right decisions. Because we believe in our conviction, it gives us strength to act on that decision. Choose friends who have similar values and convictions as you. What are your convictions? (e.g. friendships, peer pressure, finishing my education pathway, personal characteristics – integrity, honesty, faithfulness, achieving dreams etc.)

Q. Write down a personal conviction you hold and how that impacts the choices you make in that area.
For example, I have a personal conviction to finish my education pathway so that I can get into the apprenticeship I've always wanted to do. This impacts the choices I make at school; I choose to study hard in maths.

REFLECTION

Q. How can you help create a safe and supportive community?

NOTES

'CHOOSE LIFE'

strength.

SESSION SIX | HAVE RESILIENCE

outcomes.
By the end of this session, you will be able to:
RECOGNISE THE VALUE OF DEVELOPING RESILIENCE.

foundational concept... resilience.

RESILIENCE | ri-zil-ee-*uh* ns |
The ability to recover readily from adversity.

Resilience is the strength to withstand adversity. It is the ability to handle difficult situations, people, environments and setbacks. Being able to bounce back and recover from adversity makes us stronger and contributes to our dreams becoming a reality.

We need to understand that life will not always be smooth sailing. Life is not always great. Things happen that we would prefer didn't. But if life was always wonderful, would we appreciate all the great things or would we take them for granted? We can learn so much about ourselves when we go through challenges and problems. It is never comfortable when you're in the middle of adversity or challenge, but when you get through it you can look back and see what you have learnt from the situation.

Any mistakes we make are simply an opportunity to grow and learn.

resilience.

Here are some examples of how you can increase your resilience.
- Healthy relationships
- Participation
- Communication (someone to talk to)
- Overcoming problems, not giving up
- Standing up for what you believe
- Taking healthy risks
- Facing rejection or setbacks and trying again
- Not taking things personally
- Learning from your failures
- Getting information to understand what you're facing
- Adapting to new situations easily
- Being honest about your fears
- Figuring out who you are and what you want out of life, and not giving up on it
- Persevering no matter what
- Spending time with people who handle stress well.

Q. What are three ways you can work on increasing your resilience this week?

start
BELIEVING
in what you can offer.

reflection.
Write down a list of positive achievements you have accomplished and ways you have been able to help others.

_____
_____
_____
_____
_____
_____
_____
_____
_____

'I HAVE A HOPE AND A FUTURE'

purpose.

SESSION SEVEN MY POTENTIAL IS LIMITLESS
SESSION EIGHT MY LIFE HAS PURPOSE
SESSION NINE SHINE!

purpose.
SESSION SEVEN MY POTENTIAL IS LIMITLESS

outcomes.

By the end of this session, you will be able to:

RECOGNISE THE VALUE OF A POSITIVE ENVIRONMENT FOR YOUR POTENTIAL TO GROW.

IDENTIFY WAYS TO BUILD YOUR CONFIDENCE.

foundational concept.
Potential is what we are capable of becoming in every area of our life.
This can include friends, family, career, health, finances, personal character and attitude.

Our potential is limitless. Our potential is often in seed form. The seeds inside us are limitless. Each seed has potential to grow and become everything it was designed to be. The only thing that can limit us from becoming all that we can be is us.

Living in our potential requires believing in ourselves and being confident in who we are.
Our potential will not grow or be realised unless we choose to put action to it.

POTENTIAL | p*uh*-ten-sh*uh* l |
Possible, capable of being or becoming.

"Your potential is really up to you. It doesn't matter what others might think. It doesn't matter where you came from. It doesn't even matter what you might have believed about yourself at a previous time in your life. It's about what lies within you and whether you can bring it out."

JOHN C. MAXWELL

Maxwell. J.C (2007), *Talent is Never Enough*, (pg 18) Tennessee: Thomas Nelson

reflection.
Q. What do you believe about yourself?

_____
_____
_____
_____
_____
_____
_____
_____
_____
_____
_____
_____
_____
_____
_____
_____

seeds of greatness.

Here are some examples of ways we can look after our seeds of greatness.
- We nurture the seeds by valuing ourselves
- Create the right environment to bring forth the life we want – surround ourselves with healthy relationships, positive role models, and encouraging people
- Being positive and believing in our potential
- Giving ourselves opportunity to develop and try new things
- Keeping our health in balance – physically, emotionally, mentally, spiritually

Q. What are some other ways we can look after our seeds of greatness?

_____
_____
_____
_____
_____
_____
_____
_____
_____
_____

We can live our life as a garden. What grows is what we plant, and what we let others plant in it. We can choose what seeds we plant in our own garden. Seeds can be skills, knowledge, experiences, thoughts and ideas.

CONFIDENCE | kon-fi-d*uh* ns l |
Full trust: belief in the trustworthiness or reliability of a person or thing, boldness, self-assurance and poise.

Confidence comes from embracing who we are. To live in our potential sometimes requires us to step out of our comfort zone and do new things. How confident we grow is our choice. A key to living in our potential is choosing to believe in ourselves and be confident. To get something we don't have, sometimes we need to do something we haven't done before.

Q. Where is our confidence found?

_____
_____
_____
_____
_____
_____
_____
_____
_____
_____
_____

Q. Are we born with it?

Q. What are some things that can hinder you from growing in your potential?

Q. Identify the seeds in your life. What can you do with these seeds starting today?

'I HAVE A HOPE AND A FUTURE'

purpose.
SESSION EIGHT MY LIFE HAS PURPOSE

outcomes.
By the end of this session, you will be able to:
IDENTIFY PERSONAL DESIRES

DEVELOP AN UNDERSTANDING THAT YOU HAVE
SOMETHING TO CONTRIBUTE

foundational concept.

We are unique; there is no one else like us. How we are designed, our passions, our talents, and our strengths are unique to each of us and have purpose. All these qualities are in us so that we can fulfil our personal desires. There is a blueprint inside all of us. We are purpose-built and exist for a reason. There is a purpose for our life.

Discovering our purpose is a key aspect to every person's journey. We get a taste of our purpose when we tap into the desires of our heart. What satisfies us and what makes us frustrated? We each have a specific wiring with a palette of gifts and strengths that are as unique to each individual as a thumbprint!

Developing our gifts and talents, identifying our dreams and desires and learning how to use them, all help us to live a life of purpose. Purpose enables us to make a difference in our world. Life does not have to be about just living for ourselves. Our life can be used to make a difference for others.

We can choose to live in a world that is about ourselves or we can choose to include others in our world and make a difference.

reflection.

The world we live in can try to label us, put titles on us and make us try and fit into a certain box, telling us 'This is the way to be significant, popular or successful'.

In the movie 'Happy Feet', young Mumble's song was not singing, but tap dancing. This is what he was born to do, yet his behaviour was 'un-penguin' like. We all have a song to sing. We all have a message over our life, a reason for our existence, and a purpose to our life.

By being true to ourselves, we can find our heart song and use it to create a difference in the world.
In turn, others have the choice to do the same.

Q. What is your heart song?

_____
_____
_____
_____
_____
_____
_____
_____

> "When you find purpose, you find passion. And when you find passion, it energises your talent so that you can achieve excellence."
>
> **JOHN C. MAXWELL**
> Maxwell. J.C (2007), *Talent is Never Enough*, (pg 40) Tennessee: Thomas Nelson

ACTIVITY: TALENTS

TALENT | tal-*uh* nt |
A special natural ability, qualities; a capacity for achievement or success; ability; a person who possesses unusual innate ability in some field or activity.

We have each been wonderfully made. Spend some time thinking about and celebrating your strengths, talents and abilities. What we are good at can be used to help others.

What are some ways to identify talents? Ask yourself: What am I good at or what do people say I am good at? What comes naturally to me?

_____
_____
_____
_____
_____
_____
_____
_____
_____
_____
_____
_____
_____
_____
_____
_____
_____
_____
_____
_____

reflection.

Write down any dreams that you haven't been able to imagine yourself fulfilling. This can involve writing a vision statement for your life.

reflection.
Write down any dreams that you haven't been able to imagine yourself fulfilling. This can involve writing a vision statement for your life.

_____
_____
_____
_____
_____
_____
_____
_____
_____
_____
_____

reflection.
Q. Have you ever imagined yourself accomplishing your dreams?

_____
_____

EVERYONE
has strengths and talents

SEVENTY-FIVE MY LIFE HAS PURPOSE

Q. Do you most often see yourself winning or losing, succeeding or failing?

_____
_____
_____
_____
_____
_____
_____
_____

example of a timeline to achieve a goal.

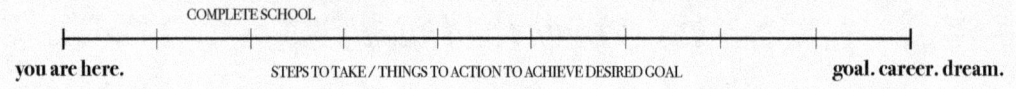

COMPLETE SCHOOL

you are here.　　　STEPS TO TAKE / THINGS TO ACTION TO ACHIEVE DESIRED GOAL　　　goal. career. dream.

goal . what you're trying to achieve.

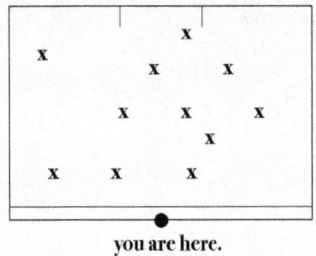

you are here.

example of how to achieve a goal.
x represents your opposition.

IMAGINE

BIRTHDAY SPEECHES

Imagine it is your birthday. What would you like people to say about you for your birthday speech? What would you like people to write about you on your birthday card?

LIKES

If you had the total approval and admiration of everyone, regardless of what you do, what would you do with your life?

ROLE MODELS

What role models do you look up to? Who inspires you? What personal strengths or qualities do they have that you admire?

CHARACTER STRENGTHS

What personal strengths and qualities do you already have? Which ones would you like to develop? How would you like to apply them?

WEALTH

Imagine you win the lottery or inherit a fortune. How would you spend it? Who would you share it with?

stick your dream collage here!
Remember: If money, time, place, ability, education and confidence were not an issue, what would you do with your life? (If you knew you could not fail, what would you do?)

watch out for
DREAM STEALERS!

FEAR
SELF-DOUBT
NEGATIVE COMMENTS
BAD CIRCUMSTANCES
LACK OF CONFIDENCE
DRUGS OR ALCOHOL
DISTRACTION
BULLYING
PEER PRESSURE
BELIEVING THAT OTHER THINGS ARE MORE IMPORTANT THAN YOU

'I HAVE A HOPE AND A FUTURE'

9

purpose.
SESSION NINE SHINE!

outcomes.
By the end of this session, you will be able to:
DESCRIBE WHAT YOU HAVE LEARNT.

Q. What do you stand for or what kind of declaration would you like to make over your life?

- I am valuable
- I am one-of-a-kind
- I am wonderfully made
- I have the power of choice
- My decisions determine my destiny
- I have resilience
- My potential is limitless
- My life has purpose

i have and will always have...

WORTH!

BODY AND SOUL, I AM WONDERFULLY MADE! I AM SOMEBODY!! I HAVE IMMEASURABLE VALUE.

I am unique, matchless and incomparable; no one in the *ENTIRE* world at present or in *ALL* the ages of time has my great gifts, abilities, heart or talents. What a woman I AM... no one has been me and no one will *EVER* be like me. Because *I AM WORTH TAKING CARE OF MYSELF*, I remind myself and the world that *"I AM A MASTERPIECE!"* There is nobody like me and there will never be anyone like me. I can't fit into anybody else's mould. I can't be compared to anyone... not even my sister, mother or friends. My *WORTH* is not related to my performance and what I do – but to my very being. My *WORTH* cannot be earned. It is inborn. I was born with this immeasurable value!!

i have and will always have...

STRENGTH!

My strength comes when I use my self-control for good, for myself and for others. Choosing safe friends, good decision-making (with my mind & not from my feelings) which empowers me to *ACT* and not *REACT*. The quality of my life is a direct result of *MY* choices. Stop. Think. Choose.

i have and will always have...

PURPOSE!

MY LIFE COUNTS. I AM UNIQUE! I HAVE PURPOSE.

I am custom made, a masterpiece, one-of-a-kind. I will be the best ME that I can be.
I have to realise that if I'm going to succeed; failing can be a part of the journey...
the important part to remember is to not stay down!

Never a failure, always a lesson.

I will learn from my mistakes and move forward.
It doesn't matter where I've been; It's where I'm going that counts!
I am able to rise above any circumstance and turn it into good!

REFLECTIONS

REFLECTIONS

REFLECTIONS

REFLECTIONS

www.ingramcontent.com/pod-product-compliance
Lightning Source LLC
Chambersburg PA
CBHW080808300426
44114CB00020B/2872